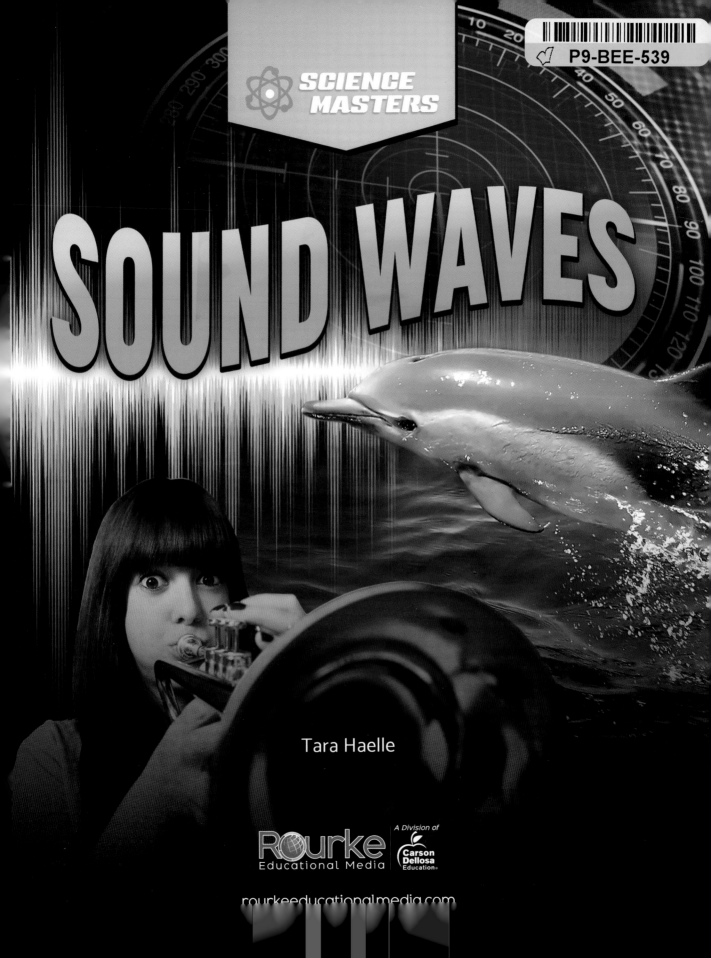

SCIENCE MASTERS

SOUND WAVES

Tara Haelle

Rourke Educational Media
A Division of Carson Dellosa Education

rourkeeducationalmedia.com

ROURKE'S
SCHOOL to HOME
CONNECTIONS
BEFORE AND DURING READING ACTIVITIES

Before Reading: *Building Background Knowledge and Vocabulary*

Building background knowledge can help children process new information and build upon what they already know. Before reading a book, it is important to tap into what children already know about the topic. This will help them develop their vocabulary and increase their reading comprehension.

Questions and Activities to Build Background Knowledge:

1. Look at the front cover of the book and read the title. What do you think this book will be about?
2. What do you already know about this topic?
3. Take a book walk and skim the pages. Look at the table of contents, photographs, captions, and bold words. Did these text features give you any information or predictions about what you will read in this book?

Vocabulary: *Vocabulary Is Key to Reading Comprehension*

Use the following directions to prompt a conversation about each word.

- Read the vocabulary words.
- What comes to mind when you see each word?
- What do you think each word means?

Vocabulary Words:
- absorb
- adapted
- compressed
- dominance
- fetus
- matter
- meld
- nerve
- pitch
- pollution
- status
- vocal cords

During Reading: *Reading for Meaning and Understanding*

To achieve deep comprehension of a book, children are encouraged to use close reading strategies. During reading, it is important to have children stop and make connections. These connections result in deeper analysis and understanding of a book.

 Close Reading a Text

During reading, have children stop and talk about the following:

- Any confusing parts
- Any unknown words
- Text to text, text to self, text to world connections
- The main idea in each chapter or heading

Encourage children to use context clues to determine the meaning of any unknown words. These strategies will help children learn to analyze the text more thoroughly as they read.

When you are finished reading this book, turn to the next-to-last page for **Text-Dependent Questions** and an **Extension Activity**.

TABLE OF CONTENTS

CHAPTER ONE

WHAT IS SOUND?

Soothing music, chirping birds, crying babies, roaring airplanes, honking cars, crashing waves, sizzling fires. Sound is everywhere in our world. Sound is a form of energy. It travels outward from its source in waves, similar to ripples in a pond after a pebble hits the water.

A busy city street is filled with hundreds of sounds all at once.

Sound energy comes from vibration, a rapid back-and-forth movement, like a guitar string's movement after you pluck it. A vibration creates a pressure wave that causes molecules to bump against each other. Molecules are particles that make up all **matter**.

Clap your hands together once. As your hands hit each other, they force out the air between them and cause a pressure wave. The air molecules closest to your hands push against surrounding molecules. The **compressed** molecules form the crest, or tip, of a sound wave.

Then the molecules spread out again, creating the low trough between waves. But as they stretch out, the outer molecules press against still more particles. The wave continues traveling outward until it runs out of energy. When sound waves run out of energy, the sound stops.

The harder you clap, the louder the sound is.

Good Vibrations

You can see for yourself how sound causes vibration. Stretch some plastic wrap across a speaker and place several grains of rice on the plastic. Turn on music and increase the volume (but not too loud!). Watch as the rice grains jump around.

Since sound comes from compressing molecules, it only travels if molecules are present. Sound cannot travel in space because it is mostly a vacuum, or an area without matter. If a space battle ever occurred like the ones shown in movies, the entire battle would actually be silent!

No Molecules

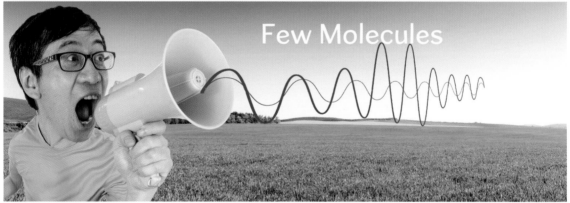

Few Molecules

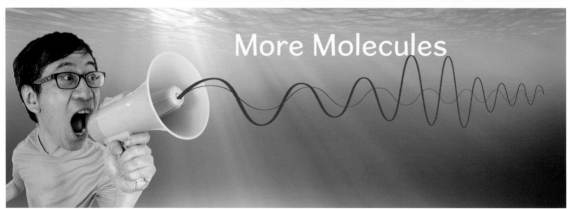

More Molecules

Sound travels at different speeds in different substances. Molecules in water are closer together than those in air, so sound travels approximately four times faster in water. Temperature also affects sound's speed. Hot particles have more energy, so sound travels faster in warm water than in cold water.

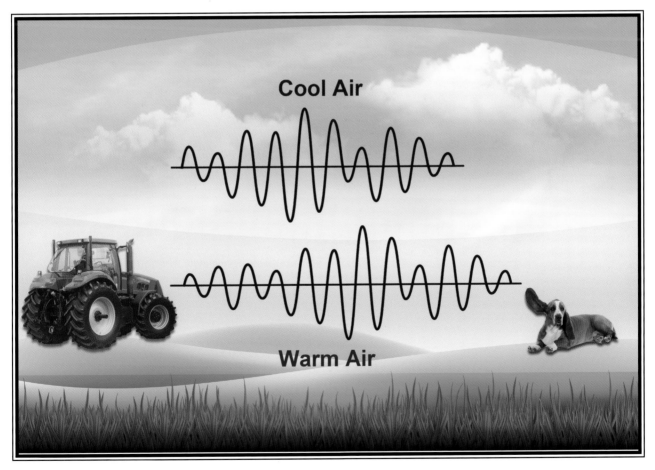

Sound travels faster in warm air than in cool air.

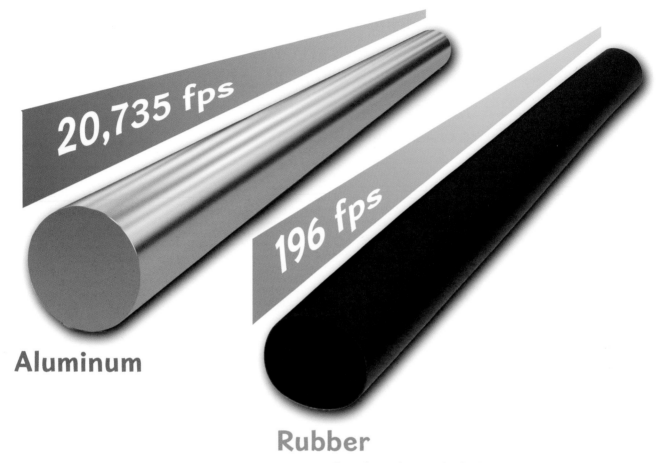

20,735 fps

196 fps

Aluminum

Rubber

Sound travels very slowly through rubber, which makes it
a good material for sound-proof insulation.

Metal also transmits sound quickly. Sound travels especially fast
through aluminum, at about 20,735 feet (6,320 meters) per second.
By comparison, at room temperature, sound travels through air at
only about 1,135 feet (346 meters) per second.

Sound waves also behave differently when they hit different types of surfaces. Soft surfaces, such as carpet or fabric, **absorb** sound waves. Hard, smooth surfaces reflect sound waves, bouncing them back in an echo.

Recording studios have walls covered with sound-absorbing materials that prevent sound from bouncing back and creating echoes.

Thunder and Lightning

Light travels faster than sound, so you see lightning before you hear its thunder. Sound takes about five seconds to travel one mile (1.6 kilometers) through air. After you see a lightning bolt, count the seconds until you hear thunder. Divide the number of seconds by five to find out how far away the lightning is. Ten seconds means the lightning is two miles (3.2 kilometers) away.

CHAPTER TWO

PROPERTIES OF SOUND

The study of sound is called *acoustics*. The parts of an acoustic wave give sound different properties. Amplitude is the distance from a wave's midpoint to its crest. A sound wave's amplitude tells how much energy the wave has, which determines its volume. Volume is how loud or soft a sound is. More energy causes a higher amplitude, which causes a greater volume. People measure the volume of sound in decibels (dB).

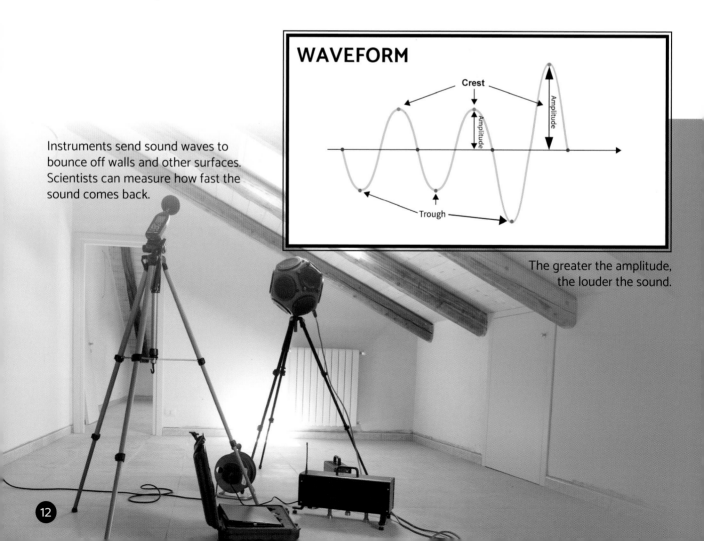

Instruments send sound waves to bounce off walls and other surfaces. Scientists can measure how fast the sound comes back.

WAVEFORM

Crest

Amplitude

Amplitude

Trough

The greater the amplitude, the louder the sound.

How Loud?

The limit of comfortable volume for humans is around 70 dB, or the loudness of a vacuum cleaner. Extended exposure to sounds louder than 70 dB can cause hearing damage. Sounds at 110 dB (16 times louder than 70 dB) cause pain, and 150 dB can rupture an eardrum.

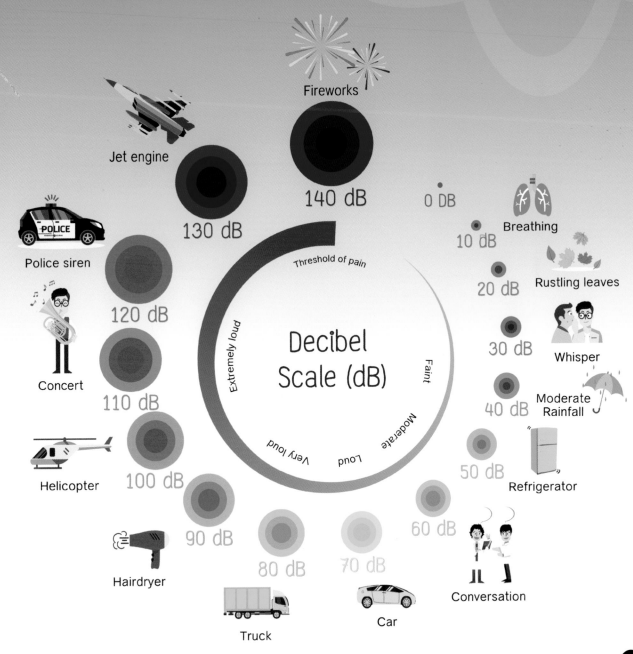

Low Frequency Sound Wave

Wavelength

Crest

Trough

High Frequency Sound Wave

Wavelength

Crest

Trough

Biggest Boom

The loudest sound ever measured came from a volcanic eruption on Krakatoa, Indonesia, in 1883. People heard its explosions, like gunshots, more than 3,000 miles (4,828 kilometers) away. It ruptured sailors' eardrums 40 miles (64 kilometers) away, and its sound waves traveled around Earth four times!

The distance from one sound wave's crest to the next is called the *wavelength*. The number of wavelengths that pass a set point in one second is a sound's frequency measured in hertz (Hz). Long, spread-out waves have a low frequency. Short, narrow waves have a high frequency.

When this Super Hornet fighter jet broke the sound barrier, it created a visible sonic boom.

Breaking the Sound Barrier

Scientists define sound's speed through air as Mach 1. Anything faster than Mach 1 is supersonic. The first person to break the sound barrier was American test pilot Chuck Yeager. He flew Mach 2 in his plane Glamorous Glennis on October 14, 1947.

Just as amplitude determines volume, frequency determines **pitch**. Sounds with a high frequency have a high pitch, like crickets chirping. A low frequency means a low pitch, like notes from a tuba. People can hear sounds between 20 Hz and 20,000 Hz. Human speech ranges from about 1,000 Hz to 5,000 Hz. The range of frequencies people can hear declines as they grow older. Children can hear high-frequency sounds that older adults cannot.

A cricket's chirping has a high frequency and therefore a high pitch.

Human conversation is only a small part of the range of frequencies humans can hear.

Many animals can hear frequencies that humans cannot. Dogs can hear frequencies above 20,000 Hz, which explains how they can hear dog whistles when people can't. Sounds above 20,000 Hz are considered ultrasonic. Sounds below 20 Hz are infrasonic. Elephants, giraffes, alligators, octopuses, and other animals can hear infrasonic sounds.

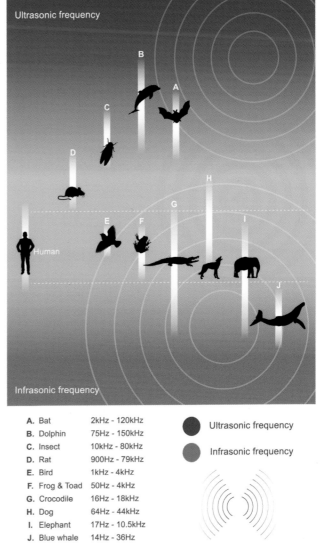

Animal Hearing Frequency Range

Ultrasonic frequency

Human

Infrasonic frequency

A. Bat	2kHz – 120kHz	
B. Dolphin	75Hz – 150kHz	
C. Insect	10kHz – 80kHz	
D. Rat	900Hz – 79kHz	
E. Bird	1kHz – 4kHz	
F. Frog & Toad	50Hz – 4kHz	
G. Crocodile	16Hz – 18kHz	
H. Dog	64Hz – 44kHz	
I. Elephant	17Hz – 10.5kHz	
J. Blue whale	14Hz – 36Hz	

Ultrasonic frequency

Infrasonic frequency

Doppler effect

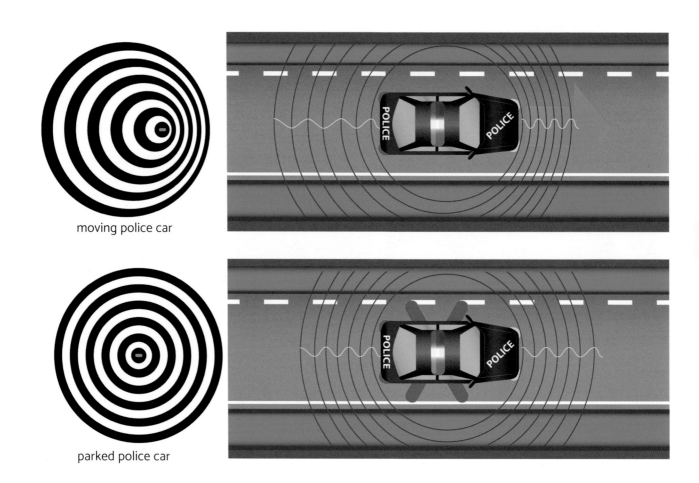

moving police car

parked police car

Frequency does not change as a sound wave travels, but it can appear to change because of the Doppler effect. When a sender and receiver of sound draw closer together, the sound wavelengths appear to get compressed, so they sound like a higher frequency.

When the distance between sender and receiver increases, the sound waves appear to stretch out, making the pitch sound lower. The Doppler effect explains why an ambulance siren seems to increase in pitch as it gets closer and then drop in pitch after it passes you.

Because of the Doppler effect, an approaching ambulance's siren will seem to have a higher and higher pitch until it passes you.

CHAPTER THREE

SOUND AS COMMUNICATION

Sound helps people communicate. Sounds like gasps, laughter, and screams express surprise, joy, or fear. But human speech is the most complex and important form of sound communication. People use their **vocal cords** to vocalize sounds and their tongues and lips to form words.

Singing requires more air intake than speaking. It also requires the singer to change the shape of the space in the larynx around the vocal cords.

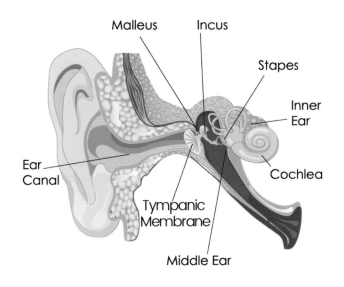

Malleus Incus

Stapes

Inner Ear

Cochlea

Ear Canal

Tympanic Membrane

Middle Ear

But how do others hear those words? Sound waves first travel through the ear canal to the tympanic membrane, or eardrum. The eardrum vibrates and sends these vibrations to the hammer (malleus), anvil (incus), and stirrup (stapes). These three small bones amplify the vibrations and send them to the snail-shaped cochlea in the inner ear.

A speaker in a large room must talk loudly for the sound waves to reach all the listeners' ears.

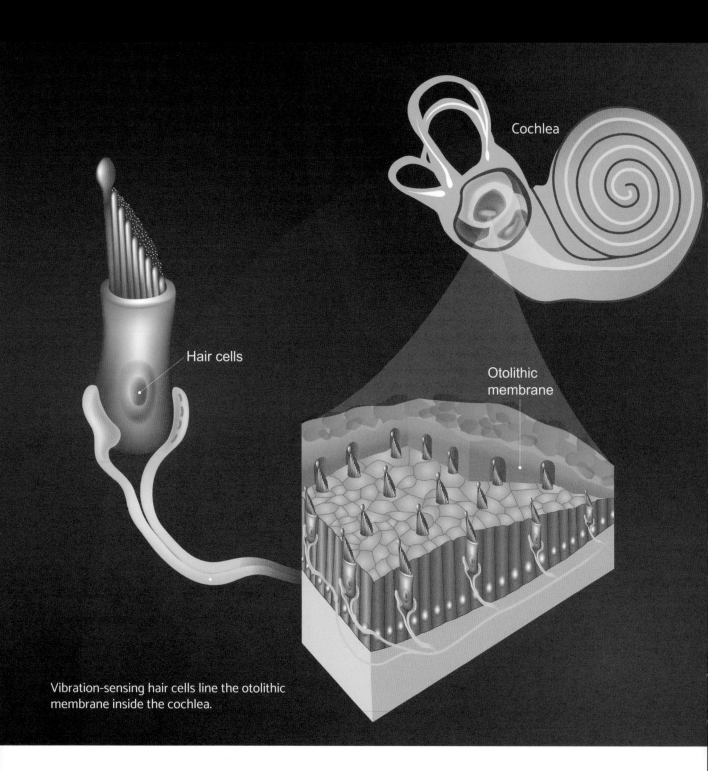

Cochlea

Hair cells

Otolithic
membrane

Vibration-sensing hair cells line the otolithic membrane inside the cochlea.

The cochlea contains fluid that ripples with the vibrations. A small wave then travels along a membrane inside the cochlea. Tiny, sensitive hairs line the membrane. When these hairs sense the vibrations, they release chemicals that create an electrical signal. The auditory **nerve** carries this signal to the brain.

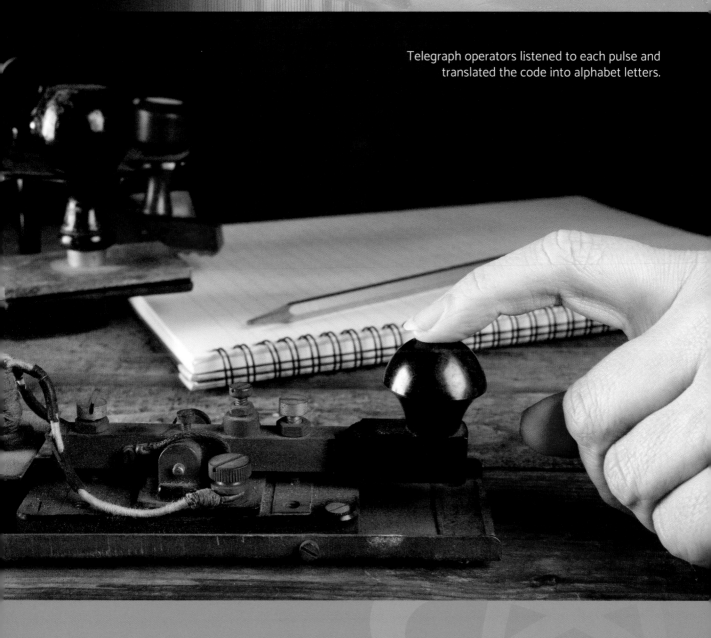

Telegraph operators listened to each pulse and translated the code into alphabet letters.

Dots and Dashes

Before telephones were invented, people used telegraphs to communicate across long distances in code. Telegraphs send electrical pulses along wires. One of the telegraph's inventors, Samuel Morse, assigned dots and dashes to the letters of the alphabet. People used his Morse Code to send messages. The best-known code is SOS, a call for help: • • • — — — • • • .

The brain interprets the signal sent by the auditory nerve. It understands word meanings, tone of voice, and inflection. Inflection describes the change in pitch at the beginning or end of a word. Someone can say, "You're funny" five different ways and mean five different things just by varying the pitch and inflection.

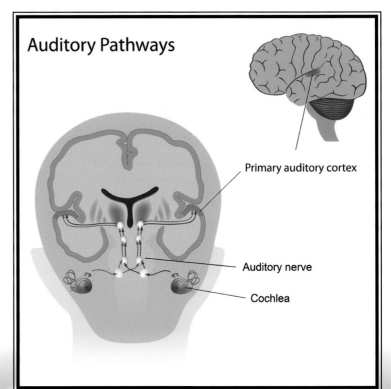

Auditory Pathways

Primary auditory cortex

Auditory nerve

Cochlea

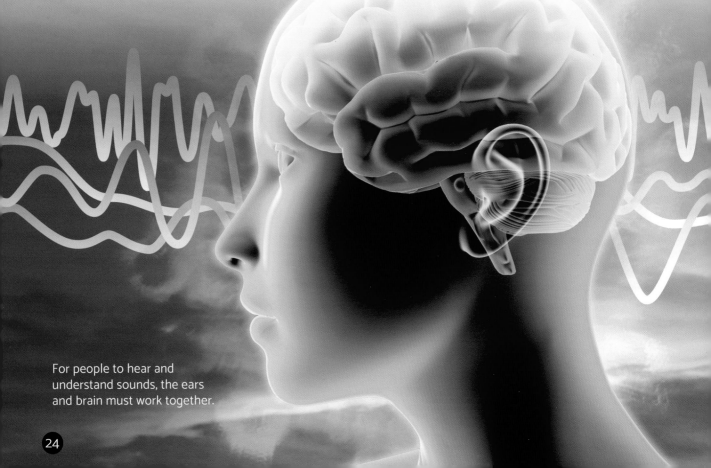

For people to hear and understand sounds, the ears and brain must work together.

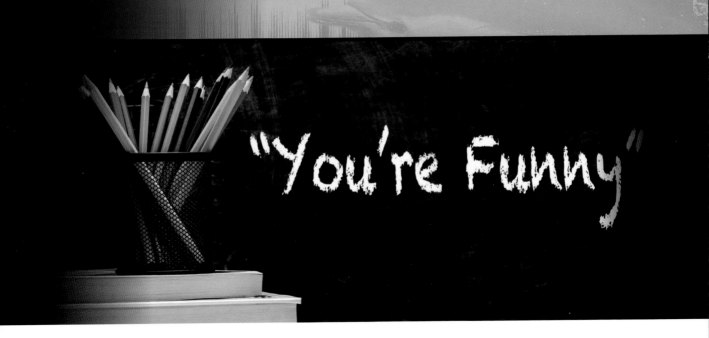

"You're Funny"

Try it! Increasing the pitch at the end of an English word makes it sound like a question. Emphasizing different words makes the meaning change too. The brain uses past learning to determine a speaker's meaning.

Sound waves lose energy as they travel, so people often use microphones to amplify, or increase the power and volume, of sound. Microphones allow everyone in a large stadium to hear a singer in the middle of the field.

Electric guitars use amplification from transducers and speakers to be heard at a distance.

Using air movement in the nasal passage, dolphins produce whistles, squeaks, grunts, and other sounds. Individual dolphins can be identified by their unique whistles.

Animals also vocalize to communicate. Cats purr to express happiness and meow at different pitches to communicate hunger, fear, or other emotions. Similarly, a dog's bark can be excited, threatening, hungry, or scared.

Elephants communicate with low rumbles that can be heard as far as six miles (ten kilometers) away.

Ultrasound and Infrasound

Many animals communicate at frequencies humans cannot hear. Dolphins, whales, bats, mice, frogs, and various insects make ultrasonic clicks, croaks, and other noises to communicate. Elephants rumble at low infrasonic frequencies, and tigers use infrasonic sounds to ward off competitors and attract mates.

Just as people clap their hands to get someone's attention or to applaud, animals communicate with other sounds too. Gorillas beat their chests to show **dominance**. Rattlesnakes rattle their tails to warn predators to stay away. Male crickets chirp by scraping together their wings to attract mates.

A rattlesnake makes its signature sound by shaking the hollow chambers found in its tail. A rattlesnake can rattle 50 times in a second. It can sustain its rattle for three hours or more.

Tiny Animal, Big Sound

Tiger pistol shrimp only grow to about two inches (five centimeters) long, but they can snap their claws shut so fast that it creates an air bubble whose pop exceeds 200 dB. The sound wave can kill animals up to six and a half feet (two meters) away.

CHAPTER FOUR

SOUND IN EVERYDAY LIFE

Sound plays an important role in people's everyday lives beyond speech and music. Sound often helps keep people safe. Some crosswalks use different sounds to indicate when to cross the street. People who are blind rely on these sounds to avoid dangerous traffic.

The first automatic railroad crossing signals were bells mounted on poles. Flashing red lights were soon added.

Hospital machines beep to notify medical staff of the **status** of individual patients. If a patient's heart or breathing stops, an alarm lets nearby nurses know right away. Police, ambulance, and fire sirens tell drivers and pedestrians that an emergency vehicle is fast approaching. Railroad crossings use loud bells to announce approaching trains.

Tornado and hurricane sirens blare across long distances to let people know to take shelter before dangerous weather arrives.

A smoke alarm's ear-splitting screech captures everyone's attention—even if they are sleeping—so they can evacuate the area immediately.

Tornado sirens can be heard 2 miles (3.2 kilometers) away.

Although sound can improve public safety, too much sound can harm health. Noise **pollution**, such as loud traffic and construction sounds in cities, can disrupt human and animal activities. Excess exposure to sounds at 80 dB and louder can cause permanent hearing damage.

If the volume is too loud, listening to music through earbuds can cause NIHL (noise-induced hearing loss).

Hearing Aids

As people age, the tiny hair cells in their ears that sense vibrations may wear out, causing hearing loss. Fortunately, hearing aids can help. These small electronic devices fit inside or behind the ear and magnify sound vibrations entering the ear so remaining hair cells can sense them.

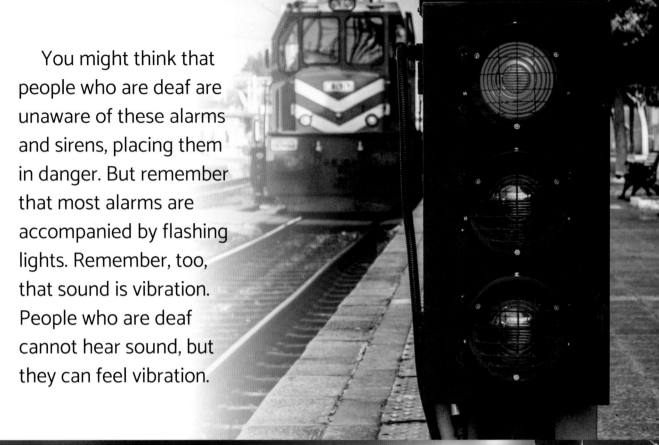

You might think that people who are deaf are unaware of these alarms and sirens, placing them in danger. But remember that most alarms are accompanied by flashing lights. Remember, too, that sound is vibration. People who are deaf cannot hear sound, but they can feel vibration.

People who are deaf enjoy music by focusing on the vibrations.

Frequencies above 500 Hz can cause a glass to vibrate so much that it shatters.

In fact, people who are deaf usually sense vibrations far better than hearing people can. Their brains have **adapted** to notice faint vibrations without the distraction of sound. Their sensitivity to vibration allows them to enjoy percussion and other musical vibrations even if they cannot hear individual notes or song lyrics.

Avalanche!

Have you heard that vibrations from loud sounds can cause an avalanche, or a toppling of snow and rocks down a mountainside? The concept makes sense, but scientists have tested the idea. Even sound waves from a loud jet are not strong enough to cause an avalanche. But sound waves can shatter glass if the sound has a frequency that is high enough and the glass is fragile enough.

CHAPTER FIVE

SOUND AS A TOOL

People have learned to use very high-frequency and very low-frequency sounds for everything from repairing the human body to finding sunken treasures. An example is sonar, a technology based on the way animals such as bats and dolphins use echolocation.

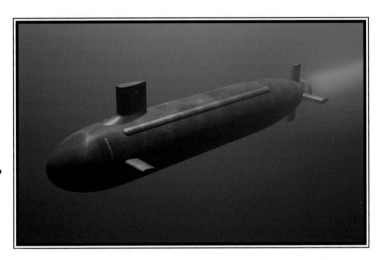

Submarines use sonar to navigate underwater.

BAT ECHOLOCATION

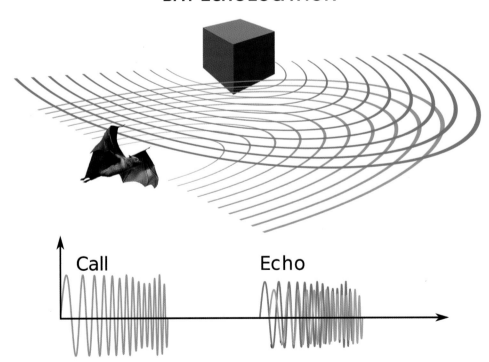

Call   Echo

Echcolocation allows whales to navigate and hunt at depths where no light penetrates.

Bats often have poor eyesight but excellent navigation. They send out ultrasonic waves and calculate the distance of objects around them based on the time it takes the sound waves to echo back. Echolocation is similar to throwing a ball against a wall and timing how long it takes to bounce back in order to measure your distance from the wall.

By constantly emitting ultrasonic sounds, bats continuously update their mental image of their surroundings. Similarly, dolphins and whales use echolocation to navigate through the ocean. Since sound travels farther in water, they can "see" long distances with their ears even in murky water.

Sonar equipment includes screens that show where things are under the water. This information comes from converting sound wave echoes into electrical signals.

People use sonar in lakes and oceans. They send ultrasonic sound waves toward the ocean floor and time their return to measure depth. Sonar has helped scientists map the ocean floor and discover objects like crashed airplanes and sunken ships.

Treasure Trove

Researchers used sonar to discover one of the biggest underwater treasures ever. The San José, a Spanish galleon, sunk in the Mediterranean Sea more than 300 years ago. But a robot using sonar helped a crew find the ship–full of treasure worth up to 17 billion dollars–more than 2,000 feet (610 meters) below the waves.

WAVE SHAPES

Analog data signal

Digital data signal

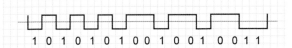

1 0 1 0 1 0 1 0 0 1 0 0 1 0 0 1 1

Amplitude modulation (AM)

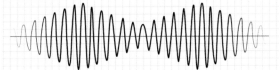

Frequency modulation (FM)

Transmitting Information

Early long-distance communication was analog, converting sound waves into electrical signals. But digitized signals are more reliable. Computers convert data into patterns of ones and zeros that electromagnetic waves can transmit. Changing the amplitude (amplitude modulation, or AM) or frequency (FM) of radio waves indicates a one or zero.

Ultrasound also aids medical care. Doctors use ultrasound to check the health of a developing baby during pregnancy. A small, handheld wand sends sound waves through a woman's abdomen into the amniotic fluid surrounding a **fetus**.

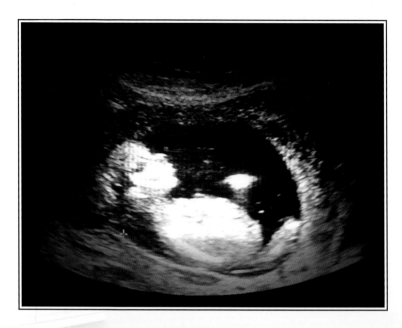

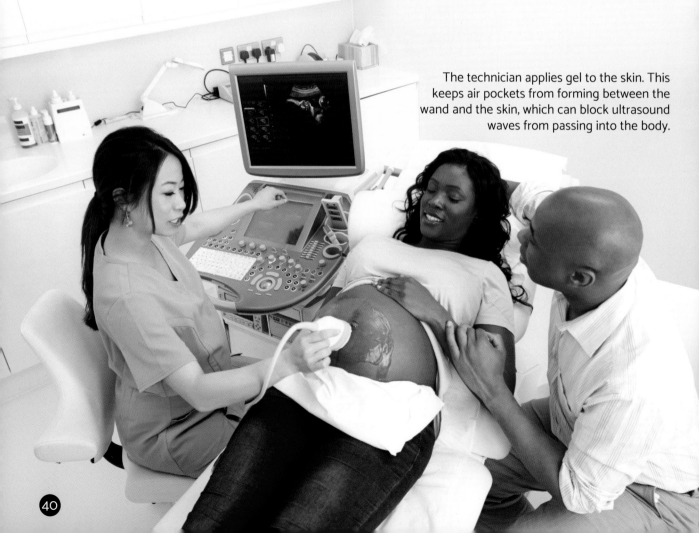

The technician applies gel to the skin. This keeps air pockets from forming between the wand and the skin, which can block ultrasound waves from passing into the body.

The waves bouncing off the fetus create an image of the developing baby, called a *sonogram*.

Ultrasound can also detect cysts, tumors, gallstones, and similar objects in the body. In fact, surgeons can use focused ultrasound, or high-intensity sound waves, to heat up and destroy tumors and gallstones. Doctors are still learning ways to use ultrasound to improve patients' lives.

A major advantage to ultrasound procedures is that they are non-invasive. No incisions or cuts need to be made.

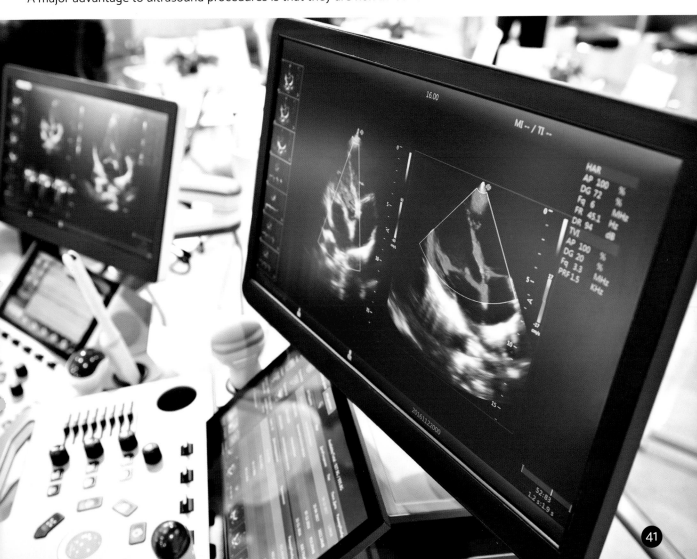

Ultrasonic sound waves can **meld** material together just as well as they can break it up. Engineers use ultrasonic waves to create vibrations that weld together plastic, metal, and other materials.

Computers, cars, and even spaceships may have parts welded together ultrasonically with a tool like this one.

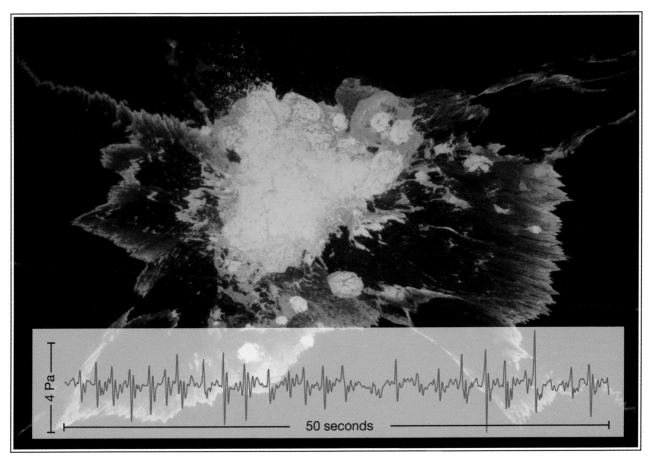

4 Pa

50 seconds

Bursting lava bubbles in Hawaii's Kīlauea Volcano create peaks in infrasonic sound waves as shown in this graph.

Scientists use infrasound—very low-frequency waves—in seismology, the study of earthquakes. They measure infrasonic waves in the ground to track far-off movements such as mining vibrations, shifts in tectonic plates, and large ocean waves.

Even if people cannot hear ultrasound and infrasound with their own ears, the sound waves are still there, all around us. Scientists continue to learn new ways to use sound waves to improve our lives.

MAKE MUSICAL INSTRUMENTS

All musical instruments create music through vibration. String instruments vibrate when strummed or bowed. Woodwind instruments such as clarinets have reeds that vibrate. The music of brass instruments comes from players' vibrating lips. Percussion instruments vibrate when struck or shaken. Use your creativity to make musical instruments from household items.

Supplies

◇ five drinking glasses with glass rims, each filled with a different amount of water
◇ clean, empty food cans with no sharp edges
◇ balloons
◇ rubber bands
◇ two pencils
◇ ten drinking straws
◇ scissors
◇ masking tape
◇ scrap paper
◇ cardboard tube from a paper towel roll
◇ beads, pebbles, or dry beans
◇ cereal box

Directions

Singing Glass: Set four glasses of water in front of you and a fifth off to the side. Dip your fingers in the side glass to lightly wet them. Carefully run your wet index finger around the rim of one glass. When you create just the right amount of friction–the action of two objects rubbing together–the glass will "sing." Try it with the other glasses to see how the pitch changes with different amounts of water.

Tin Can Drums: Stretch balloons across the tops of empty food cans. Wrap a rubber band around the rim of each can to keep the balloon in place. Use two pencils as drum sticks to play your drums.

Pan Flute: Cut off a piece of each straw so that you have ten straws of varying lengths. Arrange them from longest to shortest, aligning the bottom edges. Carefully tape the row of straws together across the top and bottom. Blow gently through the different straws to create different notes.

Shake Stick: Tape scrap paper over one end of a cardboard tube. Reinforce it with tape. Pour a handful of beads, pebbles, or beans into the other end. Seal the other end with paper and tape well. Shake!

Box Guitar: Cut a round hole about 6 inches (15 centimeters) in diameter on the front panel of a cereal box. Carefully stretch several rubber bands around the length of the box and across the hole. Strum your new guitar!

Glossary

absorb (ab-ZORB): to soak up or take in

adapted (uh-DAPT-id): changed to suit a situation

compressed (kuhm-PREST): pressed or flattened in order to fit into a smaller space

dominance (DAH-muh-nuhns): influence, control, or power

fetus (FEE-tuhs): a baby human or mammal before birth, at a later stage of development in the mother's body than an embryo

matter (MAT-ur): that which has weight and takes up space, such as a solid, liquid, or gas

meld (mehld): to blend or combine

nerve (nurv): one of the threads that sends messages between your brain and other parts of your body so you can move and feel

pitch (pich): the highness or lowness of a sound

pollution (puh-LOO-shuhn): harmful materials that damage or contaminate the air, water, and soil, such as chemicals, gasoline exhaust, industrial waste, and excessive noise and light

status (STA-tuhs): the condition of a person, situation, project, or event

vocal cords (VOH-kuhl kords): small bands of muscle in the larynx that vibrate and produce sound

Index

Text-Dependent Questions

1. What volume can start to cause hearing damage in people?
2. How can sound waves be used to create a map of the ocean's floor?
3. What is the Doppler effect?
4. What are three examples of sound used for public safety?
5. What is ultrasound?

Extension Activity

Find a place outside where you can sit safely out of the way of traffic or pedestrians. Bring a notebook and pen with you. Close your eyes for several minutes and listen to every sound you can hear. List them all in your notebook. If you don't know the source of a sound, describe what it sounds like. Then, try to learn as much as you can about each sound: How was it made? Is it natural or man-made? How far away is it? What is its purpose?

About the Author

Tara Haelle spent much of her youth exploring creeks and forests outside and reading books inside. Her adventures grew bigger when she became an adult and began traveling across the world to go on exciting adventures such as swimming with sharks, climbing Mt. Kilimanjaro, sailing the Nile, and exploring the Amazon. She earned a photojournalism degree from the University of Texas at Austin so she could keep learning about the world by interviewing scientists and writing about their work. She currently lives in north Texas with her husband, two sons, and a small menagerie of pets. You can learn more about her at www.tarahaelle.net.

www.rourkeeducationalmedia.com

PHOTO CREDITS:Cover photos: girl © Aaron Amat, sound waves © natrot, dolphin © Tom C Amon, radar © dani3315, all cover photos from Shutterstock.com; Page 4-5: istock.com | JasonBatterham, istock.com | StephenSchwartz, istock.com | GOLFX; Page 6-7: istock.com | StockPhotosArt, istock.com | monkeybusinessimages; Page 8-9: istock.com | vjanez/klagyivik/raspirator, istock.com | kiankhoon; Page 10-11: 60669919 ©Salamahin | Dreamstime.com, istock.com | coddy, ©BDPub, istock.com | PetricaR, shutterstock.com | Sergio Schnitzler; Page 12-13: istock.com. | silviacrisman, 29063049 ©Doethion | Dreamstime.com, 29063049 ©Doethion | Dreamstime.com,102089650 ©Tuksaporn Rattanamuk | Dreamstime.com; Page 14-15: Parker & Coward, Britain, 60244711 ©Mrhighsky | Dreamstime.com, US.mil; Page 16-17: istock.com | monkeybusinessimages, 44192570 ©Alexsvirid | Dreamstime.com, 102296108 ©Pattarawit Chompipat | Dreamstime.com, istock.com | monkeybusinessimages; Page 18-19: 33585459 ©Designua | Dreamstime.com, istock.com | mrdoomits; Page 20-21: istock.com | Highwaystarz-Photography, istock.com | innovatedcaptures, istock.com | snapgalleria, istock.com | kasto80; Page 22-23: istock.com | Graphic_BKK1979, istock.com | Studio-Annika; Page 24-25: 26661352 ©Alila07 | Dreamstime.com, istock.com | image_jungle, istock.com | Makidotvnv, istock.com | Nastco/goldfant/SergiyN/VladimirFLoyd; Page 26-27: istock.com | maximkabb, istock.com | Donhype, istock.com | abadonian; Page 28-29: istock.com | hypergurl, istock.com ouchi_iro; Page 30-31: 58772343 ©Chutima Chaochaiya | Dreamstime.com, istock.com | Meinzahn, istock.com | aetb; Page 32-33: fire alarm © yevgeniy11, 1992318 ©Dean Humphrey | Dreamstime.com, istock.com |Alex_Schmidt, istock.com | paolo81, istock.com | Darunechka; Page 34-35: istock.com | batuhan toker, istock.com | cookelma, istock.com | FelixRenaud; Page 36-37: istock.com | Snaprender, istock.com | CreativeNature_nl, istock.com | jamesteohart, 127651379 ©dar yati | Dreamstime.com; Page 38-39: istock.com | Graphic_BKK1979, istock.com | dani3315, istock.com | ttsz; Page 40-41: istock.com | monkeybusinessimages, istock.com | kornnphoto, istock.com | sergeyryzhov; Page 42: 100582834 ©Anuruk Charoenamornrat | Dreamstime.com, Page 43 courtesy of USGS; Author photo © Darrell Lee Morehouse III

Edited by: Kim Thompson

Produced by Blue Door Education for Rourke Educational Media. Cover and interior design by: Jennifer Dydyk

Library of Congress PCN Data

Sound Waves / Tara Haelle
(Science Masters)
ISBN 978-1-73161-469-8 (hard cover)
ISBN 978-1-73161-276-2 (soft cover)
ISBN 978-1-73161-574-9 (e-Book)
ISBN 978-1-73161-679-1 (e-Pub)
Library of Congress Control Number: 2019932314

Rourke Educational Media
Printed in the United States of America,
North Mankato, Minnesota